Contents

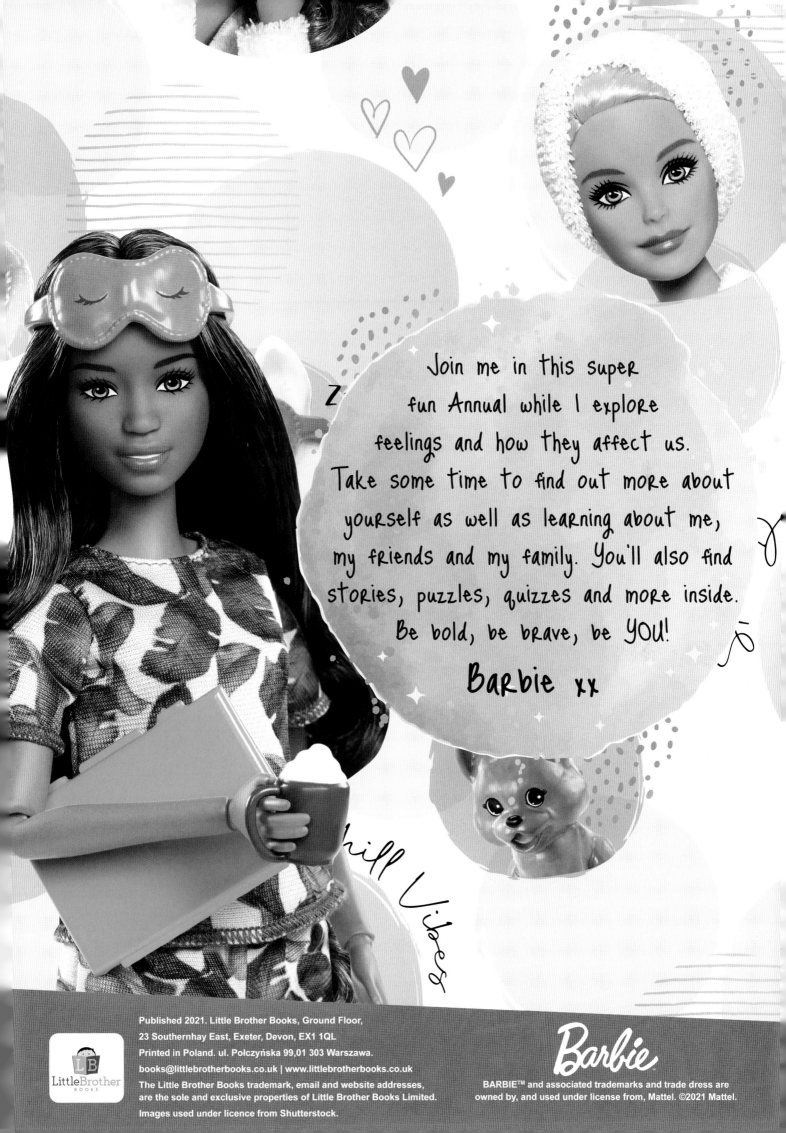

Join me in this super
fun Annual while I explore
feelings and how they affect us.
Take some time to find out more about
yourself as well as learning about me,
my friends and my family. You'll also find
stories, puzzles, quizzes and more inside.
Be bold, be brave, be YOU!

Barbie xx

Published 2021. Little Brother Books, Ground Floor,
23 Southernhay East, Exeter, Devon, EX1 1QL
Printed in Poland. ul. Połczyńska 99,01 303 Warszawa.
books@littlebrotherbooks.co.uk | www.littlebrotherbooks.co.uk

Barbie

POSITIVE ATTITUDE

It's all about PACE (Positive Attitude Changes Everything)! Have a go at filling in this page to help you see the bright side.

Three amazing things about today:

Tomorrow, I'm looking forward to:

One thing I learnt about myself:

BARBIE
'MALIBU' ROBERTS

SURF ALL DAY

After moving to Malibu when she was eight years old, Barbie quickly made friends and discovered her love of surfing. Kind, caring and curious, she loves to hang out with her friends and is always looking for new challenges and ways to share fun ideas. Her motto 'Do it anyway!' helps her be confident and strong, even when she feels nervous or scared. Nothing can stop her from having a laugh and enjoying herself!

BARBIE
'BROOKLYN' ROBERTS

POSITIVE ATTITUDE CHANGES EVERYTHING

A natural performer, Barbie loves to sing, dance and write songs. Her intense dance training has helped her take to the stage and perform dance routines effortlessly. After meeting Barbie 'Malibu' Roberts at Handler Arts Academy, she has been a loyal and encouraging friend. When 'Brooklyn' puts her mind to something, very little can get in her way. 'Malibu' has helped her learn to be more relaxed about things she can't control and to embrace life's surprises.

IN THE MOOD...
Happy

Feeling happy gives you a lovely **warm** feeling inside and makes you want to **smile**, like when a teacher tells you you've done something well or when your friend is coming for a sleepover.

DID YOU KNOW?
The body's natural 'feel-good' chemical, serotonin, can be released when you exercise.

TODAY I FEEL... CIRCLE ONE!

WRITE or DRAW
here what feeling
happy is like for you.

**YOU DON'T
ALWAYS
FEEL HAPPY;**
but **THAT'S FINE.** Just
ENJOY the **FEELING**
when you **HAVE IT**
and, remember, it
will **COME BACK** if it
has gone away.

9

READY SET GLOW

Barbie knows how important self-care is and makes time for it every day. Find the missing pieces in this totally chilled picture.

1 2 3 4 5

Answers on pages 76-77

SHHH, Don't Tell...

Secrets can be difficult to keep. Why not write them here?

FASHION FEELS

Can you fit the words at the bottom of the page in this fashion forward grid?

L
F
B

- [ ] OUTFIT
- [ ] STYLE
- [ ] LEGGINGS
- [ ] FIERCE
- [ ] BAG
- [ ] GLAMOUR
- [ ] SHOES
- [ ] BOLD

Answers on pages 76-77

MIX&
MATCH

Get your fashion on by mixing and matching these items to make the perfect outfit choices. Use different coloured pens to draw lines between each item you'd like to choose for each unique outfit.

Wild WORLD

Be inspired by nature and help keep the world wild by finding your way through this nature-loving maze.

START

FINISH

Answers on pages 76-77

SUPER SNACK

Keep snack times healthy and tasty by trying out this delicious chickpea recipe.

TIME: 20 MINS | SERVES: 1

YOU WILL NEED

- 100g tinned chickpeas, drained
- 1.5 tsp olive oil
- 0.5 tsp smoked paprika
- 1 clove garlic crushed
- 0.5 tsp chilli powder (optional)

STEP 1

Ask an adult to help you preheat the oven to 180°C.

STEP 2

In a bowl, mix the chickpeas, oil, paprika, chilli powder (if you're using it) and garlic until the chickpeas are evenly coated.

STEP 3

Spread them out on a baking tray and cook in the oven for 15 minutes.

STEP 4

Let them cool before trying your roasted tasty treat.

ASK AN ADULT
Always ask an adult before you use an oven.

ROOM FOR YOU

Ever imagine what your ideal chill-out space would look like? Well, why not design it here?

Anger

Listening to music can help when you feel angry. Write a list of your favourite songs here so you can remember them when you next feel like you want to yell at someone.

_____

_____

_____

_____

_____

_____

_____

_____

_____

Feeling angry makes us want to **YELL, SCREAM** and say things like **"IT'S NOT FAIR!"**. Sometimes we feel angry because we **FEEL MISUNDERSTOOD** or because we have been **BULLIED**.

WRITE or DRAW here what feeling angry is like for you.

IT'S PERFECTLY NORMAL TO FEEL ANGER; the IMPORTANT THING is to BE AWARE of when we feel it and TRY and DO THINGS to HELP us EXPRESS it HEALTHILY, such as EXERCISE or TALKING to someone.

DID YOU KNOW?
Sometimes taking a deep breath and counting to ten can help relieve some of the anger we feel.

SISTER HANGOUT

Time to test your memory skills! Take a look at the picture of Stacie and Skipper's bedroom for 60 seconds, then cover it up and try and answer the questions at the bottom of the page.

1 How many pictures are hanging on the wall above the steps?

2 What colour is the low table on the rug?

3 Which pet has a doggie house next to Skipper's bed?

4 How many desk chairs are there?

5 Are there pictures on the wall above Stacie's bed?

SKIPPER

 Let's do it Skipper-style!

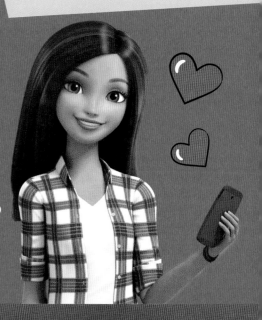

Barbie's oldest younger sister loves her independence and plays it very cool a lot of the time. Skipper marches to the beat of her own drum and likes to stay true to herself, even if it gets her into trouble. This tech-savvy sis loves music, gadgets, fashion and her cute dog, DJ, although she does also try really hard to come across unimpressed about stuff.

STACIE

Barbie's sporty sister is a true champ! In fact, Stacie is like the coach, players and crowd all rolled into one. No-one could argue that she isn't adventurous; in fact, very little seems to make her nervous or wary. She's not afraid to fail! Passion and competition motivate Stacie, which keep her mind super focused. Barbie can count on her to make dreams come true, like when she got Barbie onto a baking TV show. And the best thing is that her optimism is contagious!

Welcome to the Stacie-zone!

CHELSEA

The best littlest sis in the world!

Barbie's youngest sister is 6 years old, but Barbie considers her wise beyond her years. There's nothing that the adorable little sis loves more than playing pranks on her family and friends. As well as plenty of giggles, she also loves a tea party. Chelsea is super creative and has a huge imagination, which helps her come up with stories, like the one about the roof fairy... She isn't afraid to express herself and she's constantly finding new things to learn about.

ME TIME

Take time to make your soul happy

Unscramble these words to reveal how to make some time for yourself and find your zen.

LHICL
_ _ _ _ _

DEAR
_ _ _ _

TEDIMEAT
_ _ _ _ _ _ _ _

HERATBE
_ _ _ _ _ _ _

STRIKE A POSE

Get your stretch on by matching the shadows to the correct pictures.

A

B

C

1

2

3

WOULD YOU RATHER?

Help Brooklyn and Malibu go head-to-head by answering these questions. Say the thing that comes into your head first.

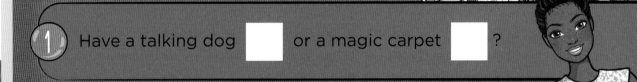

Would you rather...

1. Have a talking dog ☐ or a magic carpet ☐ ?

2. Be able to fly ☐ or be invisible ☐ ?

3. Be a famous actor ☐ or a famous singer ☐ ?

4. Only be able to walk backwards ☐ or only be able to crawl on your hands and knees ☐ ?

5. Be the funniest ☐ or be the smartest ☐ ?

6. Go to the moon ☐ or dive to the bottom of the sea ☐ ?

7. Live next to the sea ☐ or at the top of a mountain ☐ ?

8. Build a snowman ☐ or build a sandcastle ☐ ?

DREAM HOLIDAYS

One winter's day in Malibu, Barbie's mum and dad arrived home with shopping bags packed with Christmas presents for the girls. Dad wondered if they should wrap them and put them under the Christmas tree straight away to stop Chelsea trying to look for them and find out what the presents were.

"Not this year. There's no way she's finding her gift before Christmas!" said Mum.

Later that day, Ken bumped into Skipper outside the Roberts' house.

"You've gotta help. I still haven't got Barbie a present," Ken pleaded with Barbie's sister.

"I've got the same problem with Stacie," said Skipper.

So, they decided that the best plan would be to go to the mall together and help each other find the Christmas gifts that they needed.

Back in Barbie's bedroom, Barbie was hanging out with Nikki when Barbie decided to give Nikki her present.

"Barbie Roberts! You are the best gift giver ever!" said Nikki. "But I gotta ask – what's with the socks?"

"They're for our ski weekend!" replied Barbie, who was super excited about their trip together.

"I can't wait to try out my new skis. I saved for them all year. I'm packed and ready to go. All I have to do is get a great gift for Ken," said Barbie.

In the living room, Chelsea was sneaking round trying to find her Christmas presents. She looked everywhere – under the sofa, in the cupboard and even in the piano. As Chelsea lifted the piano lid, her cute pet puppy, Honey, stepped on the piano keys, making a tinkling noise. Chelsea froze!

"That had better not be you looking for presents, Chelsea," called Mum.

Outside, Trey was shouting into his phone as he held two concert tickets in his hand: "These tickets you sent me for the Static Cling Concert... They're for terrible seats! There is no way I can use these inferior tickets for the concert of the century."

Barbie and Stacie were leaving for the mall when they overheard Trey's conversation.

"You know what? I think I just found Skipper the perfect gift. You go on without me," Stacie said to Barbie.

Barbie

After Barbie set off to the mall, Stacie approached Trey and asked if she could buy the concert tickets from him.

"Pleeease! I'm a Reardon. I paid a fortune for these. Even crummy tickets are way more than you could afford." Trey replied rudely.

"Well maybe I could earn them?" Stacie asked, while quickly thinking of ways she could get the tickets from Trey.

At the mall, Barbie ran into Ken and Skipper, just as Ken was about to buy a bottle of spice for Barbie's Christmas present.

"Uhm-boog-lee-auto? That's the best spice. I bought some for all my teachers. Is that a gift?" she said to Ken, spotting the bottle in his hand.

"Nope!" he lied as he put it back on the shelf and hurried away.

Barbie struggled to find a present for Ken at the mall so decided to head home. As she looked for present ideas on the internet, she spotted an online auction to win surfing lessons. Surfing lessons would be the perfect present for Ken so she placed a bid.

Suddenly, Chelsea burst into Barbie's room and started casually snooping around.

"No gifts hidden in here," laughed Barbie.

BING! A noise sounded from her computer

"Oh no! Ugh, someone outbid me," said Barbie looking annoyed at her computer screen.

But the auction wouldn't finish for a few hours yet, so she had some time to figure out how to earn some more money so she could increase her bid.

On the landing, Chelsea carried on with her present search and found some ribbon on the floor.

"What's this? Is it for wrapping presents? Where there's gift wrapping ribbon, there are gifts!" she declared as she followed the ribbon trail.

Back outside, Stacie was working as Trey's butler to try and earn the concert tickets. She brought him a tray of different flavoured smoothies.

"Your lordship, may I perchance get those concert tickets now?" she asked in a fake British accent.

"Oh, you're a long way from done," replied Trey with a smirk on his face.

In the meantime, Barbie was baking Christmas cookies when Dad came in and begged to try one. But Barbie explained to Dad that he could only have one, no more, because she needed to sell the rest to put the money towards Ken's Christmas present.

After Skipper and Ken arrived back from the mall, Skipper decided to wrap the Christmas present she had bought for Stacie.

"Good call Ken! The Midnight Soccer Chronicles – Stacie is gonna love it!" Skipper tells Ken.

"So... I held up my end of the deal. You still gotta help me get Barbie's present," Ken pleaded. He started to worry that he wouldn't have time to get her the perfect gift.

Skipper had a think and then suggested getting Barbie something for her ski trip. Ken thought it was a great idea.

"She mentioned liking this ski jacket, but it's pretty expensive," said Ken, as he showed Skipper a picture of it on his phone.

Skipper agreed that she would love it, so Ken decided to find a way to get the extra money he would need to buy it.

Chelsea hadn't given up on her gift hunt and had followed the ribbon all the way along the landing. Weirdly, the ribbon came to an end as it stuck out the bottom of a wall.

"Huh? How can it just go into the wall?" Chelsea asked herself.

Feeling very confused, she looked at the wall, unsure of what to do next. Then, she spotted a hidden switch on the wall!

Checking to see if anyone else was around, she cautiously pressed the button. Suddenly, the wall slowly slid open and revealed a hidden room! Chelsea was stunned, but also very pleased with herself.

Meanwhile, Stacie was outside being kept busy with Trey's chores. As she pushed the lawn mower around, Stacie started to wonder if Trey would keep his word and let her have the concert tickets.

"You missed a spot... And I'm also out of smoothie. Refill!" demanded Trey

"Ugh I can't take it anymore. I quit!" she said as she marched off.

In the park, Barbie had sold out of Christmas cookies. She'd had the idea to take Nikki's bistro scooter so she could cover a larger area faster.

"Okay! Operation Skate and Bake was a success. One more batch of cookies should do it," she said excitedly.

But when Barbie turned around to leave, she saw Nikki's scooter being towed away.

Oh no, she had to chase after the tow truck and pay the fine to get it back.

Back at the Dreamhouse, Chelsea was desperate to share her secret about the hidden room with Skipper, but Skipper didn't want to know anything about the presents and where they might be hidden. She told Chelsea that she didn't want to spoil the surprise on Christmas morning.

So, Chelsea went by herself to the secret room where she had to navigate a matrix of laser beams, which Mum has installed to protect the presents.

Later, Stacie decided to give Trey a present.

"I'm still not giving you the concert tickets," he told her.

"I wasn't expecting you to. It's just something I thought you would like... Merry Christmas," she replied.

Trey felt touched that she would give him a present without wanting anything in return.

When Chelsea finally found the bag with her present from Mum and Dad in it, she said to her teddy, Dr Wiggles: "Time to find out what I'm getting from Mum and Dad."

Then, inside the bag, she saw another cute cuddly teddy bear looking at her and felt guilty when she remembered what Skipper said about waiting until Christmas to open presents.

Barbie raced home after getting Nikki's scooter back and, luckily, won the bid online for Ken's surfing lesson. When Skipper asked Barbie about Ken's present, she told Skipper about how the scooter got towed and she had to use the cookie money to pay the fine.

"So where are you gonna get the money to pay for Ken's present?" Skipper asked.

Finally, Christmas morning arrived and the Roberts' family gathered round to open their presents together.

Skipper was delighted with her present from Stacie. "Woah! Two tickets to the Static Cling show?! Awesome. Epic. Amazing... how did you ever afford them?" she asked.

"I had a little help from a friend," Stacie replied.

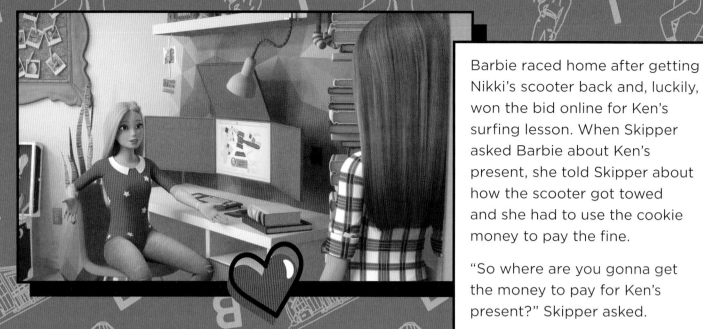

Chelsea was overjoyed with her present.

"Dr Wiggles! Look! It's your long-lost sister! I didn't even know how much I wanted one.

Thank you so much!" she said to her parents.

In future, she wouldn't ruin the surprise by trying to find the presents.

Barbie and Ken swapped presents. She gave him the surf lesson and he gave her the ski jacket.

But Ken had a confession: he sold his surfboard to buy her present.

Barbie laughed and confessed: "I sold my skis to get the money for your present!"

"I think that's the nicest present anyone has ever gotten me," said Ken.

"And you did the same for me," replied Barbie.

Then, Chelsea appeared with a big piece of mistletoe stuck on a selfie stick and they both blushed.

"It's my present to both of you," said Chelsea, cheekily.

Happy Christmas!

THE END

ALL MIXED UP

Put the scenes from Dreamhouse Holidays story in the correct order by numbering them 1 to 8.

A

B

C

D

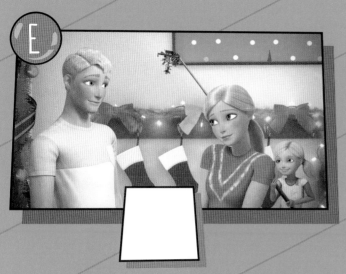

Perfect PLANET

Let's treat our planet with kindness. Find the ten words below in this earth-loving wordsearch.

- PLANET
- RECYCLE
- SAVE
- WATER
- GROW
- WILD
- KINDNESS
- CHANGE
- FUTURE
- NATURE

A	X	V	C	F	Q	W	K	D	R
H	P	J	U	I	P	O	I	F	G
L	P	L	S	Z	Y	U	N	L	W
X	V	B	A	N	M	Q	D	Z	D
S	N	X	V	N	R	K	N	W	S
D	A	W	E	Y	E	J	E	A	T
F	T	R	W	H	C	T	S	Q	Y
H	U	T	S	J	Y	D	S	Q	U
J	R	I	F	K	C	F	H	C	G
T	E	P	G	A	L	T	F	V	R
Y	Q	W	A	T	E	R	D	U	O
C	H	A	N	G	E	H	S	I	W
R	A	P	F	U	T	U	R	E	O

Answers on pages 76-77

SAVE our sea

Find the turtle that is different from the others.

A   B   C   D

E   F   G   H

GIRLS MAKE WAVES

Which close-up belongs to the dolls in the picture?

1

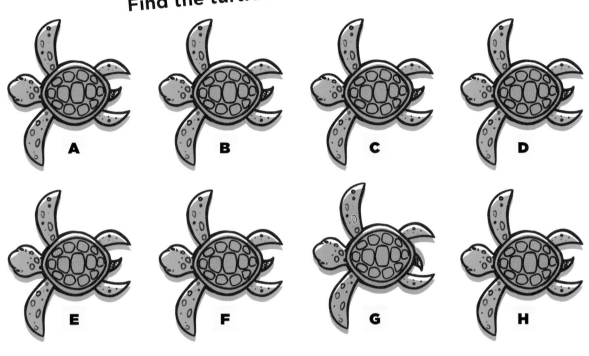

2

3

4

5

6

Answers on pages 76-77

IN THE MOOD

Sad

Feeling sad makes you feel like you might want to **CRY** or **BE ALONE**, like if your **FRIEND** has decided that they have a **NEW BFF** or if your much-loved **PET** has **DIED**.

Fill in this sadness journal for a week, by marking your sadness 1 to 10: 1 being very, very sad and 10 being not sad at all.

MONDAY	
TUESDAY	
WEDNESDAY	
THURSDAY	
FRIDAY	
SATURDAY	
SUNDAY	

WRITE or DRAW here what feeling sad is like for you.

IT'S PERFECTLY NORMAL

You might **NOT** want to **JOIN IN** with your usual **CLUBS** or **ACTIVITIES** because you **WANT** some **TIME** on your **OWN** and that's ok.

IT'S OK NOT TO BE OK.

Allow yourself time to feel sad – it won't last forever.

DID YOU KNOW?

Crying is good for you! The medical benefits of crying have been recognised as far back as Ancient Greece and Rome.

FAMILY FOREVER

There's nothing more important to the Malibu Roberts family than looking out for each other. Can you put this photo of them in the correct order?

Answers on pages 76-77

'MALIBU' MUM (MARGARET ROBERTS)

A writer-turned computer engineer, 'Malibu' Barbie's mum is unique, practical and a little bit silly. She embraces all ideas, no matter how crazy they might seem (which is good since the Roberts' daughters dream up plenty of wacky ideas!). Margaret doesn't shy away from problems; in fact, she thrives off them! Nothing cheers her up more than solving a difficult problem. She also loves keeping fit by hiking in the mountains, being a mum and watching movies. There's no doubt that she's the best role model her daughters could have hoped for.

'MALIBU' DAD (GEORGE ROBERTS)

A documentary maker and earth enthusiast, 'Malibu' Barbie's dad is inquisitive, creative and a bit dorky. George thinks he is the luckiest person on Earth – since he lives on Earth! He's obsessed by all things natural and planetary, which makes his job of making documentaries his favourite thing to do. He is constantly asking "What if...?" (which is where Barbie gets it from!) and is open to all the possibilities that the universe has to offer. Nothing can stop George from providing a constant supply of cheesy dad jokes, which makes him all the more lovable.

FESTIVE FIND

Malibu and Brooklyn cannot wait to hang out together at the Dreamhouse this Christmas. Can you spot the items at the bottom of the page in the festive scene? Give yourself a tick for each thing that you find.

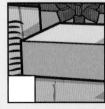
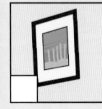

Answers on pages 76-77

FEEL THE BEAT

Colour in this picture of Daisy rocking the turntables.

GIFT BOX

Want to surprise a friend with a cute gift? All you need is this adorable gift box to hide it in.

YOU WILL NEED

- Ruler
- Pencil
- Patterned paper or card
- Scissors
- Glue
- Ribbon (optional)

STEP 1

Trace or photocopy the template on the opposite page onto patterned card or paper.

STEP 2

Ask an adult to help you cut out the box shape, cutting along the solid lines.

STEP 3

Fold along the dashed lines and then add glue to the appropriate tabs and glue in place.

STEP 4

Allow the glue to dry and then pop your BFF surprise gift inside and close the lid. Decorate with ribbon if you wish.

ASK AN ADULT
Get a grown-up to help or supervise you when using scissors

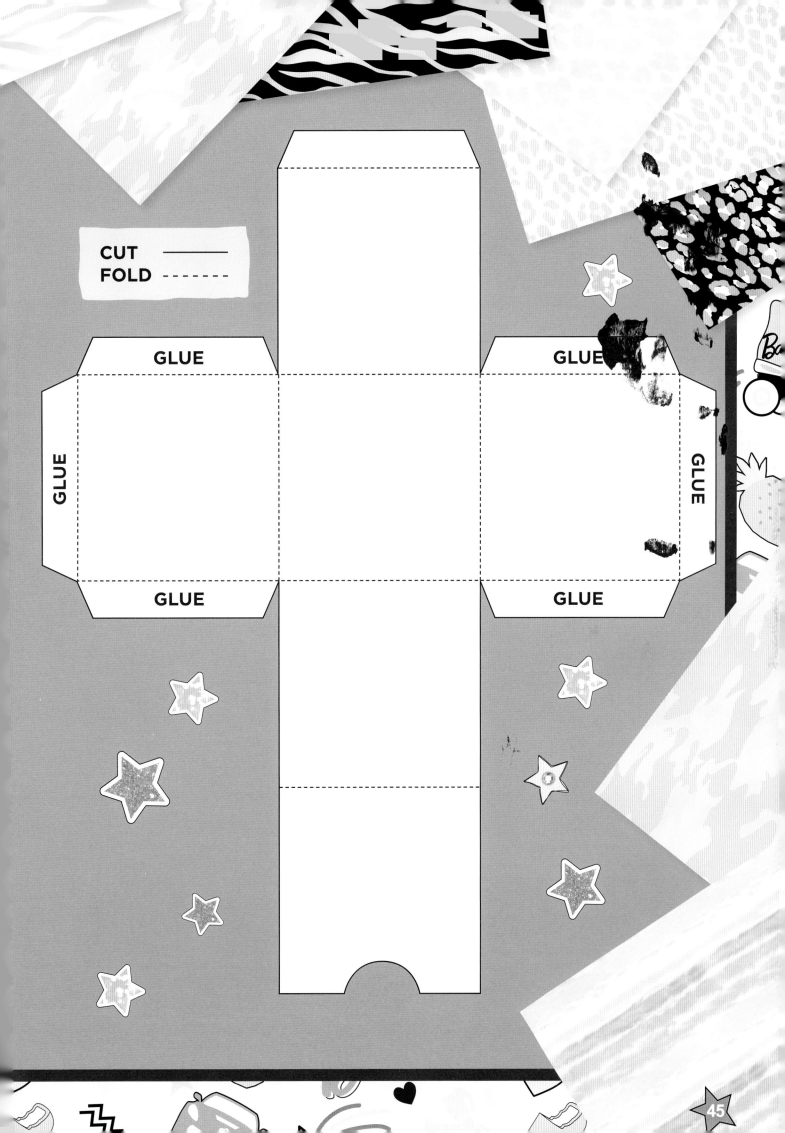

CUT ⸺
FOLD ------

GLUE
GLUE
GLUE
GLUE
GLUE
GLUE

IN THE MOOD

FEELING WORRIED can make you feel WOBBLY, SICK or even like your HEART is BEATING FAST, like on the FIRST DAY of SCHOOL or if your PARENTS are ARGUING.

Help replace some worrying thoughts with positive ones. Write three things you love about yourself here:

1

2

3

WRITE or DRAW here what feeling worried is like for you.

DID YOU KNOW?

Deep breathing can help you relax. When we breathe deeply and slowly, a message is sent to our brain to calm down.

Even though you might **FEEL ON EDGE** or like **THINGS** are **OUT OF CONTROL**, **WE ALL FEEL WORRIED AT SOME POINT.** Sometimes it **HELPS** to **BREATHE SLOWLY** or **TALK TO SOMEONE** about the things that **FEEL OVERWHELMING.**

HAPPY CAMPER

Brooklyn and Malibu are going on a camping trip with their friends. Help her write a list of things to pack here.

1. _____
2. _____
3. _____
4. _____
5. _____
6. _____

Never stop EXPLORING

Embrace the outdoors by completing these nature patterns.

A

B

C

PETS IN POSES

These pets can't get enough of the zen vibes.
Can you match each close-up to the correct pet?

A   **B**   **C**   **D**   **E**

1    **2**    **3**    **4**    **5**

Answers on pages 76-77

Barbie

YOU CAN BE A TEACHER

"Today is going to be so awesome!" exclaimed Chelsea. "I can't believe my big sister is going to be at my school all day!"

Chelsea was excited because Barbie had volunteered to spend the day helping at Golden Beach Elementary School. "It'll be great to learn more about what teachers do," said Barbie as she helped Chelsea pack her school bag.

"Hi, Barbie. It's so good that you can help out for the day," Chelsea's teacher, Miss Liang, greeted them at school.

"Chelsea is certainly excited to have me here!" laughed Barbie.

"Come and see where I sit!" Chelsea said, as she proudly showed off her classroom.

Chelsea's classmates excitedly chattered as they played with activities that were placed on each of their tables. "I love *busy fingers*," Chelsea's friend, Bonnie, laughed.

"*Busy fingers* activities develop a child's fine motor skills and are a great way to start the day," explained Miss Liang.

"I could get used to starting my day like this!"

Barbie said as she played with the colourful bricks.

The sounds of Chelsea and her friends happily playing filled the room. "Everyone is having so much fun – but how do you get the attention of a large classroom of noisy children?" asked Barbie.

"The children are great at knowing when I need them to concentrate on me," said Miss Liang, as she handed

Barbie a pretty wind chime. "Try sounding the chimes and see what happens!"

Barbie brushed the musical chimes with her hand and the children stopped what they were doing and held up their hands, to show that they had stopped their activities.

"Good morning, class," said Miss Liang to the attentive children. "We're really lucky to have Chelsea's sister, Barbie, joining us today as a special guest.

Let's give her a big, Golden Beach Elementary welcome!" Barbie was delighted as the children chorused as one, "Good morning, Barbie!"

"Let's teach Barbie our tidy-up song," said Miss Liang. The children began to sing as they quickly tidied away their busy fingers activities.

'Tidy up, tidy down, tidy away. Making things tidy for the rest of the day!'

When the tables were tidy, the children sat on a brightly coloured mat at the front of the class. "Let's teach Barbie our days of the week song," Miss Liang said to the children.

"This encourages the children to learn the names and order of the days."

Barbie joined in as the children sang the fun song.

"Each day the children have teacher-led reading, writing and mathematics," explained Miss Liang. "It's also important to cover areas such as science, personal development and creativity and to keep learning fun."

Barbie was impressed by the children's work, which decorated the classroom walls.

Miss Liang used a special projector to play a fun video on the whiteboard. A cartoon character sang a song about maths. "It's great to have modern technology," said Miss Liang. "But I still use real life objects and materials where possible."

"Young children learn mathematics by counting real objects and we have a variety of tools to help them," said Miss Liang. Some of the children were using brightly coloured shapes with different numbers of holes, while others placed buttons into pots.

Barbie noticed that Chelsea's friend, Anthony, looked worried. "I don't get it, I just don't understand," he said to Barbie.

Let's try using something different," suggested Barbie, bringing over a box of the construction blocks they'd played with during *busy fingers*.

"Let's find out what we get when we combine a group of three blocks with a group of five blocks," said Barbie. Anthony stacked the blocks together and counted the total. "It's eight!" he exclaimed. "This is fun!"

"That was a great way to explain adding groups," Miss Liang said. "All children have different abilities and they all learn differently too – a teacher's job is to make sure everyone gets the help and encouragement they need."

"Barbie, you've got to meet Miss Nibbleton, our school guinea pig" said Chelsea enthusiastically.

Chelsea filled the bottle with water and Barbie topped up Miss Nibbleton's supply of food.

"A school pet is a great way for the children to learn about caring for animals and having responsibilities," said Miss Liang.

It was time for a music lesson with Miss Laffi, the school music teacher. "We've been learning about musical terms such as forte and piano – which mean loud and quiet," she explained to Barbie. "Would you like to join in a performance?"

Miss Laffi counted and when she cued the class, they began shaking, banging and hitting their instruments in a bashing, jangling cacophony of music.

"What a fun way to learn music," said Barbie. "This kind of lesson gives children the opportunity to express themselves musically, regardless of ability," said Miss Laffi.

"I could play guitar while the children join in on percussion," suggested Barbie.

"That's a great idea!" Miss Laffi agreed.

At lunchtime, all the children wanted to sit with Barbie while they ate their lunch in the school cafeteria and they giggled and laughed excitedly. Principal Kannard visited their table to say hello. "I hope you're being looked after," Mrs Kannard smiled. "They're certainly treating me like a school superstar!" Barbie laughed.

"After lunch, the children have an outdoor playtime break," said Miss Liang. "Unstructured play is important for a child's emotional and physical development."

The children were delighted as Barbie joined them in a game of tag and they laughed as they raced around the playground trying to avoid being 'it'.

As the children dashed around her, Barbie noticed a girl sitting alone on a bench. "That's the 'buddy bench'," explained Chelsea. "It's where you can sit if you're waiting to join a game."

"Let's invite her to play with us!" said Barbie and the girl happily joined their game of tag. "What a great way to make sure no one gets left out," said Barbie.

After breaktime, Barbie and the children changed into their sports clothes for some PE. Mrs Desai, the PE teacher, led them in some fun warm-up activities. "We do jumping and stretching to get ourselves ready for the 'daily mile' jog," she explained.

"The children then run as far as they are able. The most important thing is to encourage physical activity, which creates healthy bodies and happy minds.""I'll do my best to keep up with everyone," smiled Barbie as the group of children ran alongside her.

Back in class, it was time for an art activity. "We're making an observational drawing of a flower," explained Miss Liang. In the centre of each table was a flower. "Study the shapes of the petals, and notice the different colours too," she said, as the children began to draw and paint with pencils, pastels and watercolours.

Chelsea looked frustrated with her artwork. "Drawing real life flowers is hard," she complained. "My picture looks nothing like the flower."

Remembering what Miss Liang had said earlier in the day, Barbie encouraged Chelsea to try again. "It doesn't matter how good or bad you think your picture is, as long as you try your best." With Barbie's help, Chelsea began to enjoy herself as her painting came to life. "Actually, this is pretty cool – thanks big sister!"

It was nearly the end of the school day, so Barbie and the children cleared away the art equipment while singing the 'Tidy Up Song'.

"We end each day with storytime," explained Miss Liang.

"I'd love to read to the class!" said Barbie, and the children huddled around her. As Barbie read, Chelsea thought to herself, "I have the best school ever – and the best big sister too."

★ STORY QUIZ ★

After you've read *You Can Be A Teacher*, see if you can answer the questions on these pages. Circle each correct answer.

1 WHERE DOES CHELSEA TAKE BARBIE?

- **A** Friend's house
- **B** School
- **C** Playground
- **D** Beach

2 WHAT ARE THE ACTIVITIES CALLED THAT THEY STARTED WITH EACH DAY?

- **A** Nosy knees
- **B** Twinkle toes
- **C** Busy fingers
- **D** Happy hands

3 WHAT DOES BARBIE DO TO GET THE ATTENTION OF THE CLASS?

- **A** Shout
- **B** Dance
- **C** Jump up and down
- **D** Use musical chimes

4 WHAT IS THE NAME OF THE TEACHER?

- **A** Miss Liang
- **B** Miss Daisy
- **C** Mr Lang
- **D** Miss Chang

5 WHAT SUBJECT DOES THE VIDEO HELP TEACH?

A. Science
B. Music
C. Maths
D. English

6 WHAT IS THE NAME OF THE GUINEA PIG?

A. Miss Nibble
B. Miss Nibbly
C. Miss Nibbles
D. Miss Nibbleton

7 WHAT INSTRUMENT DOES BARBIE PLAY?

A. Drums
B. Triangle
C. Xylophone
D. Guitar

8 WHAT DOES BARBIE DO WITH THE CLASS IN PE?

A. Play football
B. Star jumps
C. Running
D. Tennis

9 WHAT DO THE CLASS DRAW IN ART?

A. Flower
B. Apple
C. Toy car
D. The teacher

Answers on pages 76-77

Unlock the SECRET

Use the code breaker to reveal what Barbie and her friends are up to.

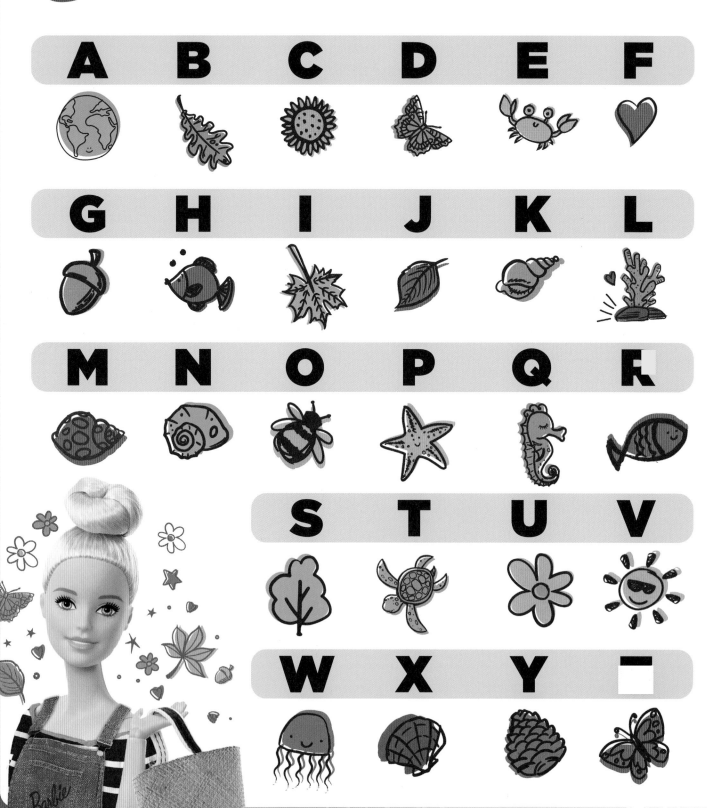

Answers on pages 76-77

MEET...

NICOLE 'NIKKI' WATKINS

Nikki is an aspiring artist and designer gifted with an eye for fashion. In fact, she'd pick out Barbie's outfit of the day, every day if she could. She's certainly one-of-a-kind with a big personality and huge amount of talent. Barbie loves that she's always full of fresh ideas, like when she came up with the idea of a surfboard cup holder. Nikki's confidence and energy won't let anything get in her way.

DAISY KOSTOPOULOS

Daisy is the coolest DJ Barbie knows and always ready to throw down a sick beat, like when she was invited to DJ at Fun Fling. She simply loves people and makes fast friends wherever she goes, which is why she belongs at music festivals. The one thing that Barbie loves about Daisy is that she is kinda unpredictable; on a road trip once, she announced "I love dinosaurs – I'm a dino nerd", which surprised and delighted her friends at the same time!

TERESA RIVERA

Teresa is a proud Latina and total brainiac. She never fails to blow Barbie and her friends away with her talent and technical genius. Barbie can always count on her to give her the best level-headed advice (as well as super scientific facts!). Teresa can also be relied on to get Barbie and their friends out of a jam. But when things get complicated in life she knows how to go with the flow.

TERESA RIVIERA
TECHNICAL TASK MASTER

NICOLE WATKINS
CREATIVITY IS HER SUPERPOWER

RENEE CHAO

Renee is Chinese-American and loves anything sporty, with a strong passion for athletics, skateboarding and skiing. She's not afraid to tell it like it is and one of the things Barbie loves about Renee is that she is absolutely fearless. Her energy is infectious and when she commits to an idea, she really goes for it. But, best of all, Renee definitely knows how to relax and have fun.

KEN CARSON

Ken is one of Barbie's very best friends. They've been friends since they were eight, so he's practically part of the family. He would do anything for Barbie and her sisters, even if it gets him into trouble. He has a passion for all things ocean-related and loves to surf, sail and dive. Being a lifeguard is one of his goals, so he's putting a lot of time and effort into lifeguard training. Fun, supportive and a little goofy, Ken can always be counted on, especially if it's to cheer Barbie up and make her laugh.

DAISY KOSTOPOULOS
TOTALLY TURNTABLE-TALENTED

RENEE CHAO
FEARLESS & FUN!

KEN CARSON
HE JUST GETS IT

ZEN VIBES

Find out your best way to relax after a busy day.

1 Your friends describe you as...
- ☐ Energetic
- ☐ Peaceful
- ☐ Playful
- ☐ Creative
- ☐ Relaxed

2 You feel your best when...
- ☐ You finish a hard workout
- ☐ You relax with yoga or meditation
- ☐ You feel sunshine and a breeze on your face
- ☐ You create something new
- ☐ You spend some quiet time alone

3 Your go-to weekend style can best be described as...
- ☐ Active, bright, bold
- ☐ Earth tones, natural, simple
- ☐ Trendy, relaxed, minimal
- ☐ Unique, eclectic, inspiring
- ☐ Laid-back, comfy, sweet

4 Your favourite genre of music is...
- ☐ Upbeat pop
- ☐ Relaxing chimes and chanting
- ☐ Rocking band classics
- ☐ An eclectic mix of indie music
- ☐ Chilled acoustic

5 The mantra that most speaks to you is...
- ☐ Always give 110%
- ☐ Inhale love, exhale gratitude
- ☐ Adventure is everywhere
- ☐ Never stop growing
- ☐ It's the little things

MOSTLY RED
Active Goddess
Your zen is bumpin' tunes, hitting the sports field and getting your sweat on! You feel most relaxed after being active.

MOSTLY GREEN
Yoga Bunny
Your zen is practising mindfulness through meditation and poses to help centre yourself and recharge your mind.

MOSTLY PURPLE
Sunday Stroll
Your zen is loving all creatures great and small. Being outside and connecting with nature helps you feel yourself.

MOSTLY PINK
Creative Queen
Your zen is letting your creative juices flow! Spending some time with your paintbrushes and pencils is how you unwind.

MOSTLY BLUE
Peace & Popcorn
Movie night is your jam! For you, there's no better way to relax than cosying up on the couch and watching your fave films.

WELLNESS PARTY

**Barbie and her friends are celebrating happy vibes.
Can you spot eight differences between the two pictures?**

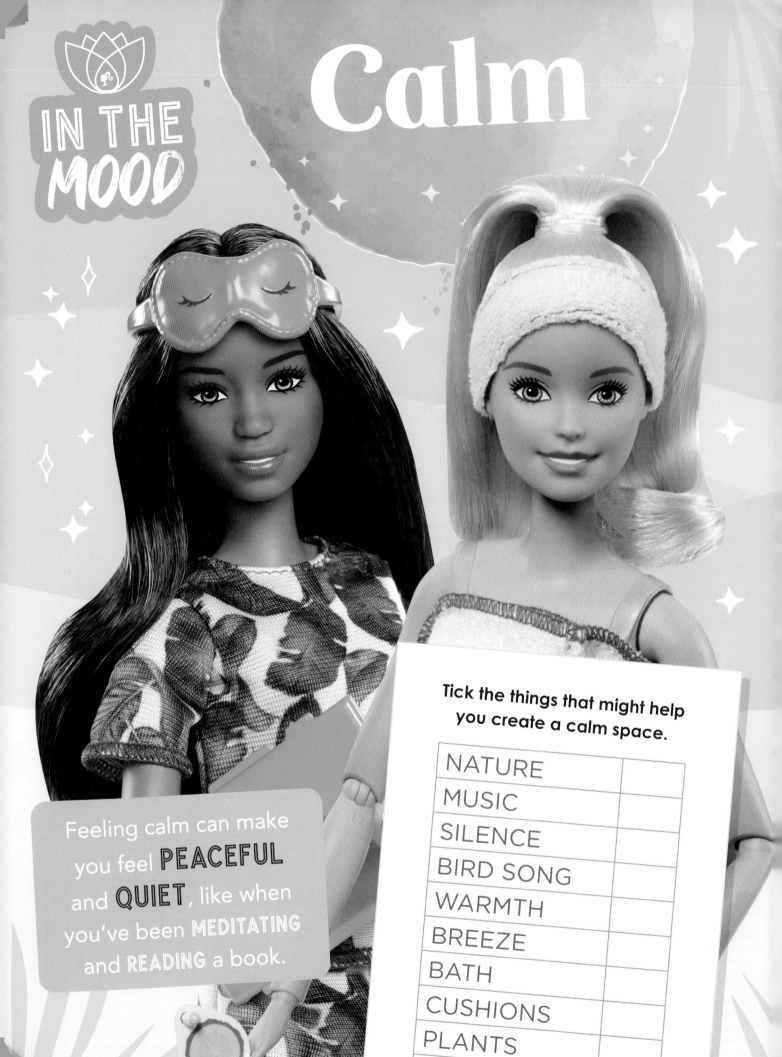

Calm

Feeling calm can make you feel **PEACEFUL** and **QUIET**, like when you've been **MEDITATING** and **READING** a book.

Tick the things that might help you create a calm space.

NATURE	
MUSIC	
SILENCE	
BIRD SONG	
WARMTH	
BREEZE	
BATH	
CUSHIONS	
PLANTS	
PETS	

WRITE or DRAW here what feeling calm is like for you.

Sometimes we can **FEEL AT PEACE** and want to do things slowly. It's **EASIER** to **FEEL CALM** by doing **YOGA** or **SLOW BREATHING**.

TRUL Y YOU

Fill in this section about yourself.

Remember a time when you were happy...

_____
_____
_____
_____
_____
_____
_____
_____
_____
_____
_____
_____

Make a list of five things you're grateful for:

1 _____
_____
2 _____
_____
3 _____
_____
4 _____
_____
5 _____
_____

Write down things you love about yourself:

_____
_____
_____
_____
_____
_____
_____
_____
_____
_____
_____
_____

HEAVENLY HAIR

Complete Barbie's hair styles by drawing accessories, such as hair bands, clips and flowers.

PUPS RULE!

Colour in the adorable pets.

TAFFY
Barbie's pup is a little shy – but is learning to be brave. She loves cuddling and nuzzling.

HONEY
Chelsea's pup is the sweetest. She loves chasing her tail and dressing up.

ROOKIE
Stacie's pup always has a plan! He loves running, jumping and being the fastest.

DJ
Skipper's pup moves to the beat of his own tail. He loves dancing and howling.

SUPER STYLIN'

Join the dots to reveal this super hairdo. Add a splash of colour, too!

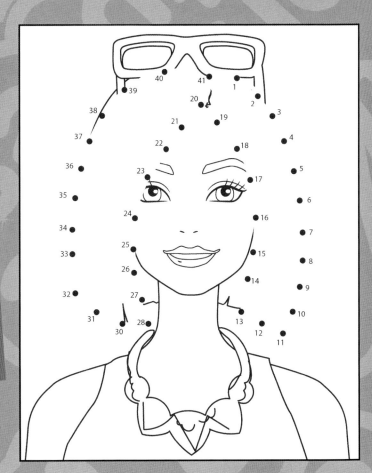

PUZZLE POP

KEY

You can move up, down, left and right.

START

FINISH

Answers on pages 76-77

Mood Journal

Fill in this mood journal to help you understand your feelings through the week.

MONDAY

Today I felt (circle one):

MORNING?

AFTERNOON?

EVENING?

Top three things about today:

1

2

3

Worst three things about today:

1

2

3

TUESDAY

Today I felt (circle one):

MORNING?

AFTERNOON?

EVENING?

Top three things about today:

1

2

3

Worst three things about today:

1

2

3

WEDNESDAY

Today I felt (circle one):

MORNING?

AFTERNOON?

EVENING?

Top three things about today:

1

2

3

Worst three things about today:

1

2

3

THURSDAY

Today I felt (circle one):

MORNING?

AFTERNOON?

EVENING?

Top three things about today:

1

2

3

Worst three things about today:

1

2

3

FRIDAY

Today I felt (circle one):

MORNING?

AFTERNOON?

EVENING?

Top three things about today:

1 _____

2 _____

3 _____

Worst three things about today:

1 _____

2 _____

3 _____

SATURDAY

Today I felt (circle one):

MORNING?

AFTERNOON?

EVENING?

Top three things about today:

1 _____

2 _____

3 _____

Worst three things about today:

1 _____

2 _____

3 _____

SUNDAY

Today I felt (circle one):

MORNING?

AFTERNOON?

EVENING?

Top three things about today:

1 _____

2 _____

3 _____

Worst three things about today:

1 _____

2 _____

3 _____

Answers

PAGE 10
READY SET GLOW

PAGE 12
FASHION FEELS

PAGE 14
WILD WORLD

PAGE 20
SISTER HANGOUT
1. 6, 2. GREEN, 3. DJ, 4. 2, 5. YES

PAGE 22
ME TIME
LHICL = CHILL
TEDIMEAT = MEDITATE
DEAR = READ
HERATBE = BREATHE

PAGE 22
STRIKE A POSE
1. C, 2. A, 3. B

PAGE 34
ALL MIXED UP
A. 3, B. 4, C. 5, D. 2, E. 8, F. 7, G. 1, H. 6

PAGE 36
PERFECT PLANET

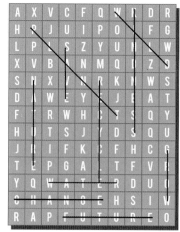

PAGE 37
SAVE OUR SEA
G

PAGE 37
GIRLS MAKE WAVES
4

PAGE 40
FAMILY FOREVER

6, 3, 1, 4, 2, 5

PAGE 42
FESTIVE FIND

PAGE 49
NEVER STOP EXPLORING

PAGE 49
PETS IN POSES
A2, B3, C1, D5, E4

PAGE 60-61
STORY QUIZ
1. B, 2. C, 3. D, 4. A, 5. C,
6. D, 7. D, 8. C, 9. A

PAGE 62-63
UNLOCK THE SECRET
TOO BUSY SAVING THE
PLANET

PAGE 67
WELLNESS PARTY

PAGE 73
SUPER STYLIN'

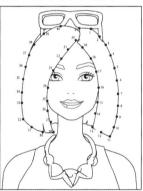

PAGE 73
PUZZLE POP

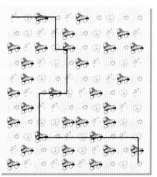